ECLIPSE ILLUMINED

POEMS & IMAGES

THOM COONEY CRAWFORD
& CATHIE SANDSTROM

ART BY
THOM COONEY CRAWFORD

TEBOT BACH • HUNTINGTON BEACH • CALIFORNIA

A Tebot Bach book

Tebot Bach, Welsh for little teapot, is a Nonprofit Public Benefits Corporation, which sponsors workshops, forums, lectures, and publication. Tebot Bach books are distributed by Small Press Distribution, Armadillo and Ingram.

The Tebot Bach Mission: Advancing literacy, strengthening community and transforming life experiences with the power of poetry through readings, workshops and publication.

for Will and for Elizabeth
and to all those who carry the light

Though the leaves are many, the root is one...
> —W.B. Yeats

The dark hours of my being...then the knowing comes...
> — Rilke

TABLE OF CONTENTS

ABOUT ECLIPSE ILLUMINED

These 17 paintings on paper 15" x 11" came into existence in 2010, on my return from living on the southwest coast of Ireland, on the Ring of Beara. The series rose from a lifeline heralding oval spheres with their eclipsed faces, where fractional moments conjoin mythic archetypal reverence. The inward eye lifts from the phenomenal to the numinous—Beauty's wonder. This hidden mystery out from the cosmic womb from a universal selfhood is alchemy in its quest for a dynamic harmony.

—**Thom Cooney Crawford**

These poems speak to the images and to each other in a poetized dialog where, as Thom would say, "the heart level illuminates." Together, we sequenced the images, then collected our poems in response to the paintings. Last, we sequenced the poems to create this journey inward and outward. Ekphrasis has always appealed to me, even though it is often difficult (if it's ever possible) to capture the ineffability of art in language. One learns by trying to breathe the incongruous wonder.

—**Cathie Sandstrom**

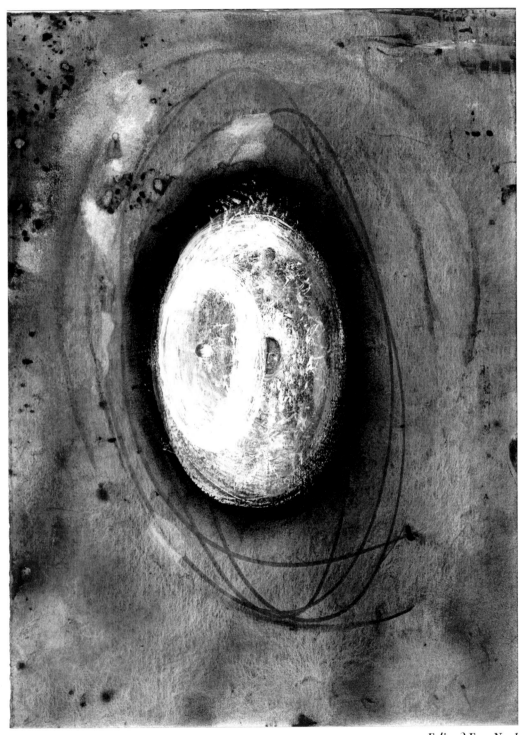

Eclipsed Face No. 1

A Trick of Light

Spear, scoop, reamer, wire —
on the table in the sculptor's studio.
Knurled handles flecked and sticky with wax.

Low rays of sun gild the river,
the meditating Orpheus on the wall.
Forehead, cheek and closed eye — gold.

His other eye — scarified, cloaked
in blue injury darkening to dream.
Indent of his third eye, shadowed.

✽

Seen from the kitchen's louvered window,
the elm's bare branches are limned gold —
first light slow-flowing down

until the sun's high enough to catch
the tulip poplar. Suddenly: *day*. The room's
dust motes swirl in Brownian motion until

they drop from view, blinking on and off
like quantum particles — as Orpheus
returns to bronze, color of earth.

✽

Drawn inward and down into ourselves,
how we are each called to witness.
Awakened, and if we are lucky,
redeemed.

✽CS

Lashed by Light

Star beams intersect
Lashed by light.

Dawn has no gravity.
Tapped by a pollen hand

I had no other instrument
To laminate my response

Other than an Orphic lyre.

*TCC

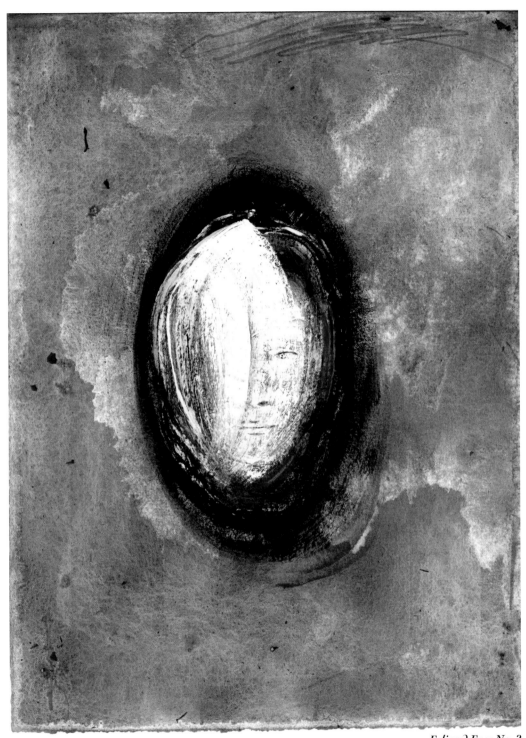

Eclipsed Face No. 2

Presence

Wax oxidized   looks   like bronze
On every surface   I see   imprint of   thumb/ palm/ fingers

Almost as tall   as the sculptor   *Or-*
pheus   returned from   the Underworld

A pillar of paradox: scarified eye   raked   shut
     the tines   pulled   down   the cheek

     The lidded   eye   closed
     in   Peace   *Or-*
     Tranquility   *pheus's*

Delicate   sculpted cheekbones   Lips
together   not pressed   Unlike   the arms

folded   tight   at the sides   Under   the   rippling
     Shroud   Swaddling   Or-

Cocoon   Fist-sized   chest depression
suggests   heartless/openhearted   Either

and both   Surrounding pool   of slow-moving   time   Or-
Pace   the artist matches   crating it   for   transport

The hollow-hallowed   gallery   waits

In   the   empty   studio
Pall   of silence   as of smoke   a haunting

Orpheus   looks out through   unfinished   pine slats
Power   held captive   by tentative   agreement

I ask   how   can   you   sleep   *Or-*
pheus   in the next   room   crated

The sculptor   says   *What you see*
     rising   *leaking out:*   *his anima*

*CS

Realm of

In the realm of
Looking for the summit

That supersedes
The mind's curfew

That is set to the
Vanishing objects,

Nature's fertility
Hits my head

Like a feather
With a spoke

Of light —
I circled life.

Metamorphic chant
Ingested.

More than a flash
Of a sound bite,

The unfettered truth
With a kinship

Of caring preserves.
Streaks of luminous

Love, and
The soil of our

Numenon nature
Is life, being sacred.

*TCC

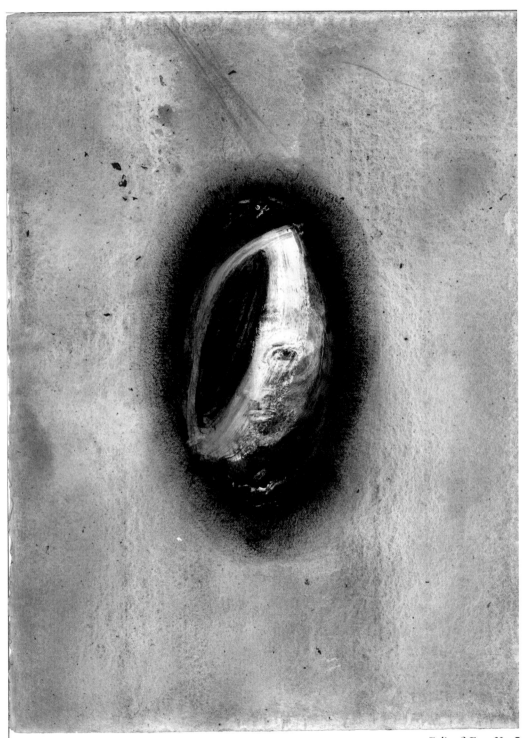

Eclipsed Face No. 3

I Forge

Affording with some cut out stammering
Bestrewn in the hygiene of words
That lacked in forwarding to a magical verve,
I have come now to feel poetry
By its induced innocence
Being more real in the astonish appeal,
Than the collected dust scattered around my traveling feet.
I am drawn to words quickening to point beyond

As I go toward the muses that silently mystify to inform,
As I forge to transform melancholy into a growing tree
Not slurring optatively, I leap closer to become a burst of glow.
I cannot be wrong having heard this ripening rise

Above modality's tease,
And above those wranglings I tussled with, to reify.
I am drawn to the frameless field of lilies,
Music that has ears, barley breath of landscape bodies,

And what grooves in me is to be aware, with an earth feel
That keeps the planet's expression close to an emotional horizon.
Hidden in the song words, I keep inverting to discover its belong,
Sung at twilight at the borders of the changing night into first light,

Where the muses are found gathered at the gate,
Waiting to decide what are to be the most profound verses to let through.
While they discuss astrophysics and the intuition for advancing,
I slide past them, luminously with a love song, before they renew.

*TCC

Ark

*In 2015, the Oxford Junior Dictionary cut forty common words, all relative
to the Natural world, replacing them with terms of the virtual world.*

Willow   Minnow   Mussel   Lark
Dropped.

Acorn   Adder   Otter   Fern
Not used enough to merit an entry.

Singled out for loss —*Raven*.

> *I have to build,*
> the sculptor says,
> *what I need*
>
> *to protect*
> *these wax creatures*
> *I keep bringing*
> *into the world.*
>
> His *Orpheu*s series,
> each one expressing
> the metaphor slightly
> slant

Why we need
starling, wren.

I lie awake, worry about
linnet, fen, hallow.

*CS

Eclipsed Face No. 4

Grew from Root

I grew from root
Into an arc of comprehension
Ripened from the tree I came to know.

I grew into a disembodied transmutationist mediator.
The last phantom through the night
Scurried away.

Within a taut silence I took on an eye of an arrow
Made from the first enlightenment
Taking flight on a non-thinkest act

To crystallize an accuracy
Aimed to cross over both an end and a begin.
Railing wild, I became surprised.

Something in me was off-kilter
Conjecturing,
Pitting, into a spurious separation.

I turned to see behind me,
Stoked to a new intensity,
Orpheus playing the lyre

And I listened
As if it were the planet's wing of song.
Magically, it released the intrinsic in me.

*TCC

Cire Perdue

Fr. Lost Wax

For structure and stability he builds
an armature. Then warms the wax

his fingers press onto it, modeling
the fine features of his Orpheus,

poet and prophet transformed on his
return from the Underworld's darkness.

Whole days, weeks, spent shaping
and re-shaping the delicate face —

sensuous lower lip, the aquiline nose.
One eye's closed in serenity.

Or peace. The other — scarified.
Deep gouges disfigure the cheek.

 For the sake of truth, the artist, capable
of perfection, turns on his own creation.

Are we not also marked? What can
we understand of our own

disfigurements shaping us?
What if, rather than masking scars,

we bold-burnished our wounds,
became more visible, more whole.

*CS

Eclipsed Face No. 5

Pulse of the Seed

Puffed clouds disappear as you rake the sky in your eye.
Blue winds, like invisible bodies, are on cyclical spins
And the imagination surpasses the strategy there within.
Some take watch to those archaic stones wearing thin
To bend the thought of time backwards, to etch a new forward

Where the will of expression serves as a lead way.
The mighty likeness hewn in airy pollination
Prompts us to feel inside the dawn-dipped reverence
Intake experience.
Life wills, hearkening the same, to what deems significant.

And the black hole admits light
By our self luminous sight, life wills expression.
While the cosmic music is recorded, sublimating
The lambent twilight that soothes the melancholic dreamer.
Life's rise is to reach for what we seek, but first undo, to recognize.

Daunting it is for the least way juggler.
Daunting it is for the diminishing word on the stone cutter.
Newly feelings long to give shape
To what can exonerate.
Keepers of wisdom reappear, having had many names to be called by.

Keepers of seers of star clusters reappear having had many faces to be looked at.
Seers who seize the task to awe, inspire, reappear to sing love's instillment
Bear it out, see behind the scarred and the beautiful earth salutations.
Life's rise from the bittersweet regrows on a maximum demand for liberation.
Regrowing on a manifold of finite procedures, seers seize life from awareness.

And the oak's bardic song, clearly is still of long, in the radiant cosmic tree.
The ancient survivability in us retrieves what lasts,
Listens to the music in the pulse of the seed.
Liberation is not on one's sleeve, it's the heart of thee, who sees.

*TCC

Translating Light

Held up a million miles away from us,
a six-meter mirror's gold honeycomb face

catches low radiant light, images from
billions of years backwards in time.

Invisible infrared translated into visible
color my mind's eye translates again:

> *An ocher mountain range spangled with stars.*
> *Ova at the threshold of a stellar nursery.*
> *A red Valentine; a blue birthing.*

Things I can't grasp: distance (a million miles);
time (13.5 billion years ago); Lagrange points

(earth and telescope held
in lockstep as they each orbit the sun).

I stand at the sink, tap running, holding
in both hands a cantaloupe mysterious

as the Earth. My fingertips questioning
its Braille rind. All the ways

I am blind.

*CS

Eclipsed Face No. 6

The Painting

The painting is on the wall.
You may stand in front of it
Look right at it
Turn your thoughts around it.

Sit inside, feeling it.
Breathe in its atmospheric aroma,
See into its fusion of starry worlds,
Follow the sapphire lines

Down its sensual swelling curves,
Hear the visceral music inside its deep
Color of purring blue
And then, slide back into

A calmly ease
Absorbed by your light,
Being that you lit the painting alive
From its dead matter.

The alchemy of what occurs
Is inherently of you
Beyond the frame of thinking —
It is the transcendent view.

*TCC

Because I Wanted to Know What the Painting Sounded Like on the Inside

Standing before it, I open the painting,
step inside to hear the rushing

of hollowed-out wind because
this universe is not static.

From the threshold, I look out on arcs
of light drawn into spheres spinning,

crossing my field of vision in trajectories
straight and curved. Pinpoints of light

illuminate a darkness that accords
everything in it the space it needs.

The artist, his back to me, dips his brush,
in slow motion draws his hand across

his body then raises his arm, extending it as if
reaching out for some Adam, any Adam, flinging light

from himself, his hand, his brush out over
the universe he's creating; the light traveling

in a low arc, front fringed like a cresting wave.
I dare not step off —

uncertain I could get back. I ask
is there gravity in the painting.

Without turning, the artist speaks. *Yes, but no
falling. Only attracting forces and arrival.*

Those who pass through
have only come home.

*CS

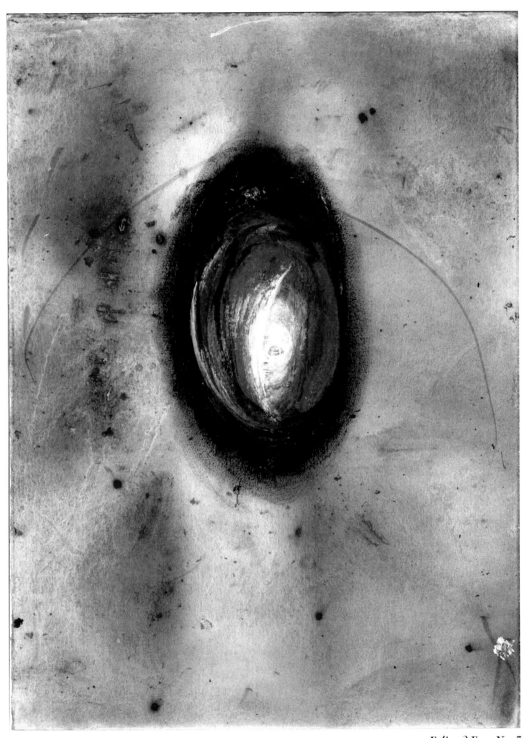

Eclipsed Face No. 7

Equinox

Plain as the panes of a penniless
chapel, this room's four panels
of diamond-patterned leaded glass

streaked yellow-green, as if
two colors of molten glass were
poured together but unstirred.

On this September afternoon
for over an hour they glow warm
and rich as saffron, pour light

onto a quartet of bronzes
each centered before a panel.
Primal as gods: the four elements —

Fire, Earth, Air and Water —
dark against the glass until
that liquid hour when the sun

re-enacts the crucible's flow.
Come from fire, in shadow they hold
cold secrets. But backlit and warmed,

they speak of alchemic power:
base material refined to bridge
the body's core to pure spirit.

*CS

Changing Markings

The changing Markings
Found in the clay

We do indeed, dance on.
Eruptions appear

In rage, become nature's
Way of sculpting

The earthly maze.
Having left the dusted

Earth feet to its retreat,
I now follow the star charts

Redrawn from the heart.

*TCC

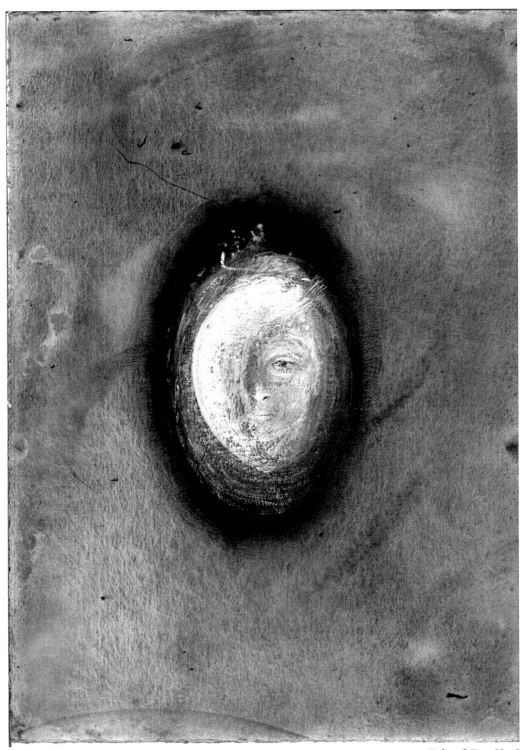

Eclipsed Face No. 8

Flutter

Off the rushing
Tides

Your mind is such
A flutter, fluttering

Come back
Come back

To the pure water
And go upstream.

*TCC

In the Sculptor's Studio

Once in its presence
No going back

The armature within
hums like marrow in my bones

Implicit invitation
Unbidden   it enters me

My palms ride the arc's current
flowing back to the sea

Grasp the curve and it takes hold
Useless to name it

Only retreat
to a time before language

Most ancient form
of enchantments

Oneness

*CS

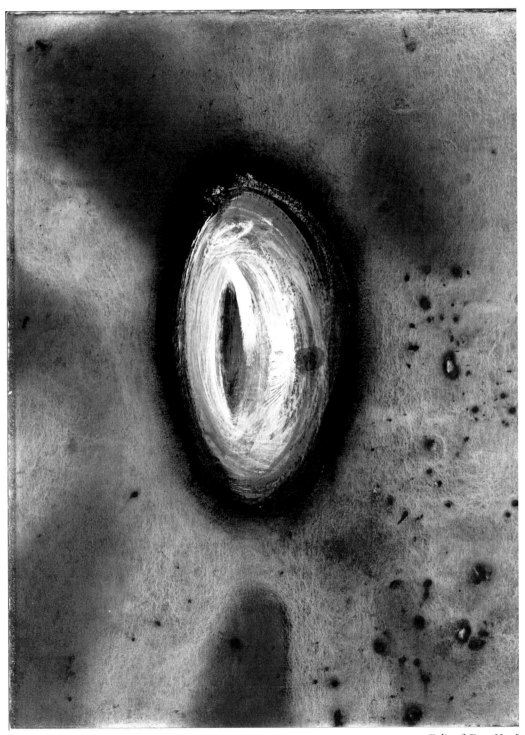

Eclipsed Face No. 9

Tilting Head

Tilting head, I wear you
Solemnly, as I learn
To position perception

On the end of a light beam.
From a long dream
I have stepped into the telescope

Of the mind, to watch
The faces, as orbs in their design
With a pliability to wax, and then

Wane, never the same,
As the lunar stratagem patently
Confers, while lovers continue

To be bearers of the steady gaze.
For even the given intensity
Of seeing fulfills

Expression of the heart Eye.
Seers know
That dawn every morning

Is telling you that you are the light
Of its preexisting songs.
Your solar eye shine is never not on.

Lovers never erase what lasts,
Emanating one, excavating
The symmetry that defuses the aghast.

*TCC

A Viewing Platform

Orbiting at 66,000 miles per hour, our earth spins
skeins of our past so thin light passes right through.

Like the spun glass *angel hair* we once spread
on the tree at Christmas, layers of this diaphanous

veil diffuse and suffuse — an enveloping gauzy swath
of past over which unimaginable futures will settle.

Riding the planet like a child on a carousel,
I stand in a whirl of color. My gaze penetrating

at times two layers at once, stopping on a single
face, our eyes locked in a moment of knowing

instantaneous   eternal   fleeting.

*CS

Eclipsed Face No. 10

Unitive Astonishment

Poetry dashes past the spectral tides
In the reeling feeling on a deep sigh,
Strikes a pause on a beautiful form

In the likes of what attracts,
Vermeil mountain,
Misty mysterious waves of incandescence.

Then, poof, the mountain moves dreamily
From the frame of your perception.
Objects of the beautiful come and go,

Different moods, different pleasings,
Different eyes see different infatuated patterns,
Satisfying different palates.

Only what is incapable of vanishing
Remains. And there are those poets who correlate
Keat's timeless hymnal.
Beauty is Truth,
Truth Beauty.

Emblazoned rhapsodic flash,
Something deepens within the well of being,
Beauty's intrinsic origin.

And the poets continue to corollate,
Enchanting us to this unitive astonishment
That we constantly return to, to feel our divine fertility.

Some may think this is digging up
An archaic language from some period that chimes.
Don't let fashion's clever harangue fool the likes of you.

The awe that comes from beauty's rise
Is the most unstained spontaneous surprise,
Shaking your innermost, to quiver you out from mind's time.

*TCC

November Morning

I crept into the studio an hour before sunrise
to be where the painting and sculpture happened,

touched everything—each tube of paint, every brush,
the feathers and rags he used, his sculpting tools.

Walked around works in progress—20 paces around
Circle of Life, its sweeping arc 10 x 8 x 3 feet.

The figure in the base birthing the rising figure
evoked memory: my son leaving my body in a rush.

An hour later the artist brought coffee, listened
while I struggled to wrap language around

what his art caused to rise in me.
We sat at a small table. *Stop using*

your objective mind, he said.
This is purely experiential.

I stood where I was destined to be.

*CS

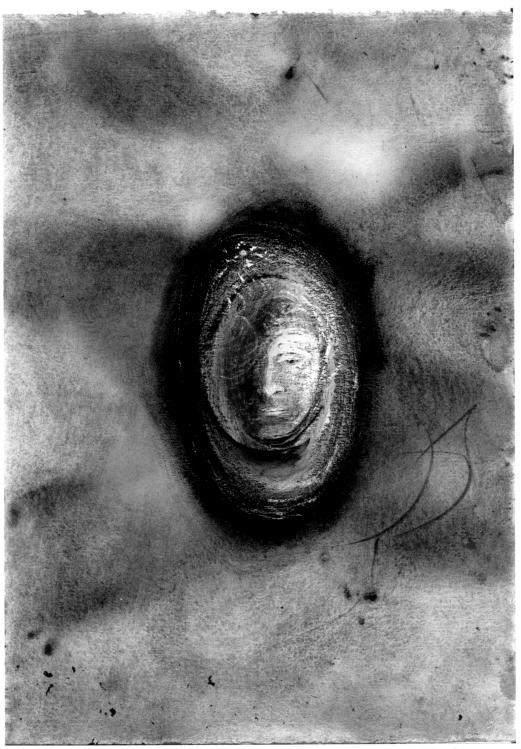

Eclipsed Face No. 11

Twilight Smile

Further than living on a long shadow,
Further than an irretrievable look,

Inspiration concedes to voice, an inside faith
On a dimensionless light, hidden in the arc of art

That can make the oracular language palpable.
Shifting hues manifesting on the enigmatical face.

Sheer instinctual unshaken aura-sown feelings,
Gestating off the pearly vibration

Like water rings on the harp. Effortlessly
The music preserves the muse, who enchants.

Slight curve of knowing pressed upon her lips,
Lunar look, with a lucent halo influence.

Who is this Venus?
Who is this Mona Lisa?
Who is this Madonna?
Who is this Woman with a pink?

Slow, deep, moving, hush blush of resplendency,
Without time's transmutation.

Peacefully, she is silencing to the eternal duration
Of her unnamed glance, intimately luminous.

And what can mystify the world, holding it to wonder,
Is in her twilight smile.

*TCC

Winged Messenger

A pair of red-tailed hawks ride the thermals
from the valley floor up the face of this hillside.

My mind, swept clear of all intention, follows
their turning gyre, spiral in the sky. They climb

the wind, sail without effort on a stream
that Nature, in her generosity, provides.

A sign from the spirit world —
intuition awakening insight.

Hawks, lend me your keen-eyed vision:
whole sight flowing into sharper focus. Let me

also soar, trusting the wind under my going,
borne up by the ways we connect.

As you and I step off the precipice of the known, you,
love, in passing, lay a feather on the page I'm writing.

*CS

Eclipsed Face No. 12

Twist, Turn, Reverse

She waved her song around me
Whispering into my ear.
The earth is in my eye.
The cipher vision has a porous appearance.
I lay out the stones around the garden,

Build up the wood pile by the house.
String yarns onto verses
That yarn balls unravel, to thread into tales of what was.
Render in charcoal, the old black and white portraits
And as I try to dust them, the dust becomes the fading faces.

I paste on the collage patterns that hang the ideas
To the outside look, reflecting through the spectrum of desire.
I was drawn into words that are bygone ways from story lines
And she whispered into my ear, as I was waiting for dawn.
Blood red flow boiled inside one body to another.

Twist turn reverse reflect be born having been,
The ever I am, is more than a quest in the head.
Is more than a walking voice.
Is more than a brain charged when plugged
Into the phenomenal floor socket

While inside my eye the earth images keep flying in orbit.
And in some atavistic surprise, some ancient idea
Wants me to keep running down to the same shore
For another life's round.
And what lasts after the blast?

You cannot live fully by just ringing charm bells.
Something peaceful stays to brave those innovations
Registered in some of the muted memories.
Counting a billion in currency was affixed to somebody's craze.
Even in my mouthpiece, the soul needs to find expression.

I lay into her breath of surety.
I am converging with her through this beautiful inlaid harmony.
The touch of touch that radiates is in the response of generosity
Spiraling back to reawaken the primacy of the heart's constancy.

*TCC

This Thin Line of the Present

where past and future confront
each other is the threshold of all else —

every learned or felt thing. It all
happens here: the inner and outer

vying for balance as this line advances
relentlessly toward the unknowable

while the past — part refugee, part
asylum seeker — hauls behind

its bundles of memory and circumstance.
The task of refining takes place here

in this narrow, but expandable, present:
the dark *prima materia* of our lives

transformed into a lantern held high
to illuminate one step   then the next.

*CS

Eclipsed Face No. 13

Rhapsody

The mystery may stiffen the voice first.

The herd may cast you out to reel on a flat causeway.

Deep mythic sigh,

Something mysteriously is revealed behind the phenomenal display.

She in her rebirthing mood sent me the way back

To the mythic tree.

*TCC

Empathy, the Dark Side

What is it about a shattered
pane that begs the hand to trace

jagged edges? Someone
else's loss allows me

to approach my own. The way
I save broken things

I will never be able to mend:
a wound I thought had closed.

A temple bell, struck, resonates
all through the garden.

Not that the heart can't hold
but rather, that it can.

*CS

Eclipsed Face No. 14

Elder Swift

Like a tree we grow toward.
Suddenly
We are an elder.
Cerebellum spread on the diadem

Of the greying head,
Wearing its proper look,
Leaves of skin, autumn's pulling
Color wind.

Sculpted shapely column
Curving
Upright, with knotted branches
That entwine

The mind, the rooted hand,
The palm of the tree.
A nascent spirit listens to my call.

A dryad matron offers her voice
With the lyrical reinstalled.
She took me for a cosmological spin,

Elder swift, soul steering.
What do you see in the dark?
Flash on a fallen star,

Toward its spaceless begin,
Twinkling formulation tingles
On the sensation.

Heliocentric rhythmic inhalation
Sprouting into an improviser,
Off the confluent, where all my

Growing has been to arouse wonder.
What I found established never left.
Art's fired up universal recovery

Is from nature's wonted arrangement.
I am inspired by her attained beauty.

*TCC

Before

Each day's   rife
a step into   the un-guessed-at

The quotidian present   rushes
to fill the void

landing on what only
seems   solid

After loss   the heart's
stubborn   elasticity

bides   every sorrow

Ready and expectant   the mind
rests   lightly

above the clanking
engine room   of the brain

The soul   on some days
wingless   on others

        anything

in that   particular   moment
before my foot
                touches down.

*CS

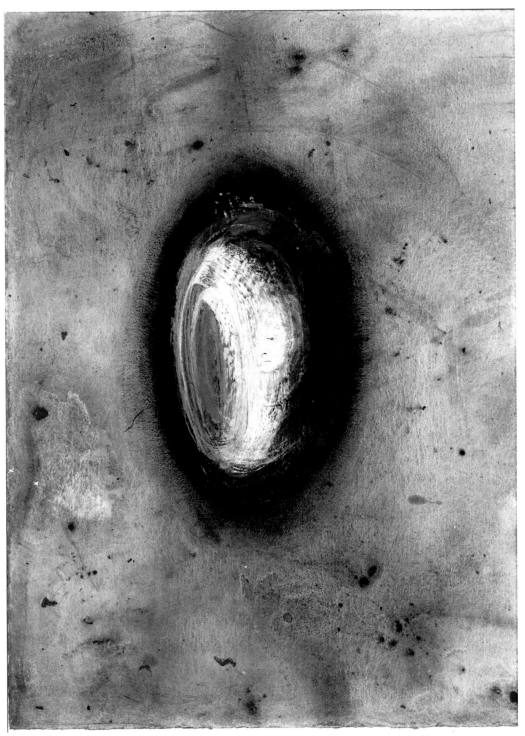

Eclipsed Face No. 15

Attend To

The upsurge of it is
The seedling from the cogency
On the pneuma,

East facing on a generative ancient
Devotional conversion;
What I was born to attend to constellates.

Springing enough harmonies,
Welcoming beauty's unforgotten splendor,
Following the four winds

Assures that a melodic response
Points to what draws life to its genesis.
Like the first seed sound where poets

Roam the interiority seeking to reveal
The primordial relaunch.
Extraordinary outburst, ensuing

From love's knowing, unflinching
Beyond whirling, the numinous
Eradicates the fractional.

For this truth of home is beyond time,
For the light of being
Outpours from the divine.

Oval moon arrests my eye.
The inevitable propels me
To follow the luminous sign.

*TCC

The Living and the Dead

after John Berger

In the center of a vortex
of light, spinning filaments
surround me. We touch
at times, you and I —
an imperfect exchange:

that sunset, how I knew
with certainty those gilded
edges of cloud defined
a shoreline — the lake of light
where you now live.

Three months later, seeing
a painting so like it, I knew
the artist had depicted
not only where you are,
but where I'm headed.

If I am in the core
of time and space and you
are in the surrounding timelessness,
then I have lost you
in my dimension only.

*CS

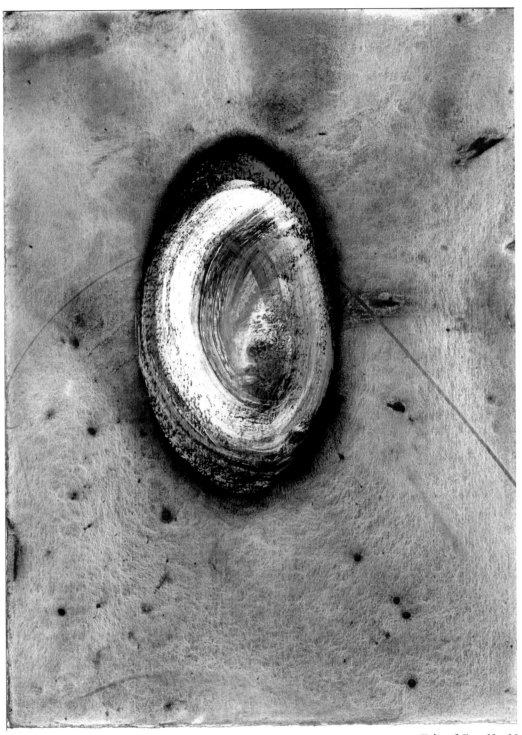

Eclipsed Face No. 16

The Body So Compact

Bone, organs
shot through
with vessel and nerve
packed tight

against taut skin.
Any breach causes
a rupture. Unlatch
that stuffed valise —

no space to slip in
anything. But

what if the body's
more like a Chinese puzzle?

Flip the case over,
it opens again,
threshold of the mind
a fractal of the inner

life of the cosmos:
galaxies slow-wheeling
their long dazzling arms
around a core of light.

*CS

Willow Wind

Round around sound in your
Befitting voice, speaking through

The moon's influence,
Releaser and increaser,

Echoes heard off wounded sighs.
Hush, hush and the willow winds cry

Wearily as everything not tied down vanishes.
Planet's wing of song suddenly consecrates.

The earth elements receive angel frequencies,
Where there is no stopping on the thinly

Motive, nipping away, contracted on
A bondage in oblivion's den of disbelief.

Having sat at the reptilian mislaying dark trance
Are you not ready now to open your clear eye?

This time as the luminous draw is to look within,
What is usurped by its disharmony dissolves.

When it comes from transforming from the bestiality
To the divine, fully interceding, to reclaim the right perspective,

Vision's recovering is in the revelatory feelings that now are reset.
Adhering to the illuminating self that conveys the nascent forms.

Wing, wing, resound that bring the innerly to awake,
Travels through the cosmic womb, on enlightenment's way.

Oh, rightly so, peace prevails, willow winds grow into songs,
Recognized, is what prompts the sublime, off nature's life flow.

°TCC

Eclipsed Face No. 17

Obeys Light

The eclipse deepens
Lifelines

Arranged in some
Forms to ignite,

Awe struck
By discovering

The oldest face
of the universe.

Are you the wearer
Of the speed of light?

Wondrous condensed
Archetypes speak this.

The constant self—
Consciousness has no
Gravity,

Obeys light.

*TCC

Benediction

with a line from Rilke

In the silence after the door
is slammed, before the guttered
flame yields to dark —

the nails, bitten, the letter
written and mailed, the hidden
painful past hung out

on the line to dry in the rain —
after the years of waiting,
the knowing comes

so quiet   and so simple.

*CS

"Hoisting Up the Innermost," Sculpture
Image No. 18

One More Wish

from the precipice

where I stand:

that when I step off,

I am borne up.

*CS

Waking

Dew drop, clay feet
Effortless
Is the open heart

*TCC

Cathie Sandstrom is a Los Angeles-based poet and writer. Her poems appear online at the Academy of American Poets (poets.org) and have been published in *The Southern Review, Ploughshares, Lyric, Ekphrasis* and other leading literary journals. Anthologies include *Coiled Serpent* and *Wide Awake*, among others. Of two nominations for a Pushcart prize, one was from *The Southern Review*. Her poem "You, Again" is in the artists' book collection at the Getty Museum, Los Angeles and at the University of Southern California. Two of her poetry manuscripts have been finalists in several prestigious book competitions. Her essay "Braiding the Dreamscape" was published online by the C.G. Jung Society of St. Louis, and her essay "Getting Broken" appears in *Master Class: The Poetry Mystique* by Suzanne Lummis. Her writing on veterans' issues was published online by the Huffington Post for six years. Presently, she writes for the National Veterans Foundation and is currently working on her second and third novels along with poetry. A military brat, she has never been "from around here" and still expects to hear from the Pentagon any day.

❈

Thom Cooney Crawford, painter/sculptor/ poet, earned his MFA in painting at Syracuse University and did graduate work in sculpture at the Rhode Island School of Design. He began his 40-year career in New York with two back-to-back shows at Tibor De Nagy gallery. He's had 34 solo shows, 16 of them in New York City, and his work has been exhibited nationally and internationally. A recipient of an NEA grant, New York CAP Grant, Open Studio Award and Cill Rialaig Residency Award, he has taught at Middlebury College, Parsons School of Design, Binghamton University and Lafayette College. In the early 2000s he left the art world, college teaching and the U.S. to "clear the bramble" from his head. He lived first in Bavaria, then for four years on Ireland's wild west coast on the Ring of Beara. On his return in 2010, he went into his studio and worked in isolation for a decade until his most recent one-person exhibit "The Inner Eye of Art / The Outer Spark." His poem "Flutter" was published in _Chronogram 2019_, and he is the author of _Raising of the Heart_, a visual novel (published under the name Thomas M. Cooney). He relocated his home and studio to the Los Angeles area in 2020. His art can be seen at **www.thomcooneycrawford.com.**

❊

TEBOT BACH
A 501 (c) (3) Literary Arts Education Non Profit

THE TEBOT BACH MISSION: advancing literacy, strengthening community, and transforming life experiences with the power of poetry through readings, workshops, and publications.

THE TEBOT BACH PROGRAMS
1. A poetry reading and writing workshop series for venues such as homeless shelters, battered women's shelters, nursing homes, senior citizen daycare centers, Veterans organizations, hospitals, AIDS hospices, correctional facilities which serve under-represented populations. Participating poets include: John Balaban, Brendan Constantine, Megan Doherty, Richard Jones, Dorianne Laux, M.L. Leibler, Laurence Lieberman, Carol Moldaw, Patricia Smith, Arthur Sze, Carine Topal, Cecilia Woloch.

2. A poetry reading and writing workshop series for the Southern California community at large, and for schools K-University. The workshops have featured local, national, and international teaching poets: David St. John, Charles Webb, Wanda Coleman, Amy Gerstler, Patricia Smith, Holly Prado, Dorothy Lux, Rebecca Seiferle, Suzanne Lummis, Michael Datcher, B.H. Fairchild, Cecilia Woloch, Chris Abani, Laurel Ann Bogen, Sam Hamill, David Lehman, Christopher Buckley, and Mark Doty.

3. A publishing component to give local, national, and international poets a venue for publishing and distribution.

Tebot Bach
www.tebotbach.org